Life's BIG Little Moments

FATHERS &
DAUGHTERS

Life's BIG Little Moments

FATHERS &
DAUGHTERS

SUSAN K. HOM

STERLING

New York / London
www.sterlingpublishing.com

For my father, William, with love

STERLING and the distinctive Sterling logo are registered trademarks of Sterling Publishing Co., Inc.

Library of Congress Cataloging-in-Publication Data

Hom, Susan K. Life's big little moments : fathers & daughters / Susan K. Hom.
      p. cm.
  ISBN-13: 978-1-4027-4317-7
  ISBN-10: 1-4027-4317-3
1. Fathers and daughters. I. Title.
  HQ755.85.H6342 2007 306.874'2--dc22

                                     2007012382

10 9 8 7 6 5 4 3 2 1

Published by Sterling Publishing Co., Inc.
387 Park Avenue South, New York, NY 10016
Distributed in Canada by Sterling Publishing
c/o Canadian Manda Group, 165 Dufferin Street
Toronto, Ontario, Canada M6K 3H6
Distributed in the United Kingdom by GMC Distribution Services
Castle Place, 166 High Street, Lewes, East Sussex, England BN7 1XU
Distributed in Australia by Capricorn Link (Australia) Pty. Ltd.
P.O. Box 704, Windsor, NSW 2756, Australia

Printed in China

Sterling ISBN-13: 978-1-4027-4317-7
     ISBN-10: 1-4027-4317-3

For information about custom editions, special sales, premium and corporate purchases, please contact Sterling Special Sales Department at 800-805-5489 or specialsales@sterlingpub.com.

Cover and interior design by 3+Co. (www.threeandco.com)

Introduction

Daughters see their fathers as heroes who chase monsters away
and know how to fix practically everything. Fathers may not always
know all the answers, but they usually know where to look.
Whenever their fathers are around, daughters feel safe and loved.

In turn, fathers see their daughters as heroines who brighten
any room with their smiles and show compassion for others.
Daughters are determined to learn how to ride a bike—
no matter how many times they fall down. Fathers are proud
of their daughters' inner *and* outer beauty.

Their bond is a special one that only strengthens over the years—
from delightful piggyback rides to the bittersweet Father of the Bride
dance. Fathers and daughters aren't perfect, but they do continually
learn from one another. In all of life's BIG little moments, fathers and
daughters inspire each other to live with love, courage, and joy.

Daughters teach fathers

to enjoy reading out loud.

Fathers help daughters

turn the pages.

Fathers know

when to let daughters

take the lead.

Daughters can't help

but make fathers smile

from ear-to-ear.

Fathers show daughters

how to build the best

snowman on the block.

Daughters inspire fathers

to become boys again

while playing in the snow.

Daughters depend on fathers
to tell a good bedtime story—
complete with sound effects.
Fathers reassure daughters
that there are no monsters
under the bed.

Fathers run alongside their daughters' bicycle—

ready to catch them

if they fall.

Daughters teach fathers

to stay determined

and keep trying.

Daughters tell fathers

that they love being tossed in the air.

Fathers reassure daughters

that they will always land safely.

Fathers help daughters

stand tall.

Daughters remind fathers

that shoulders can be

the perfect perch.

Daughters show fathers

that even a meal of mashed peas

can be cause for celebration.

Fathers encourage daughters

to be enthusiastic.

Fathers teach daughters

that each day is full of surprises.

Daughters help fathers

pick out the right pumpkin.

Daughters ask fathers

to tell silly jokes.

Fathers encourage daughters

to share about their day.

Fathers hold daughters

like the whole world

is in their hands.

Daughters remind fathers

how fun Saturday mornings

can be.

Daughters show fathers

how to love animals.

Fathers help daughters

take care of their first pet.

Fathers challenge daughters

to pursue excellence in

everything that they do.

Daughters inspire fathers

to never stop learning.

Daughters remind fathers

to be curious about new things.

Fathers show daughters

the beauty in simplicity.

Fathers help daughters

reach new heights.

Daughters teach fathers

that life is a balancing act.

Daughters squeeze

their fathers' hands tightly.

Fathers help their daughters

keep their balance.

Fathers show daughters

that hugs are wonderful gifts.

Daughters remind fathers

to slow down sometimes.

Daughters rely on fathers

for a boost every now and then.

Fathers help daughters

attain what seems out of reach.

Daughters show fathers

how to have a blast on the dance floor.

Fathers help daughters

keep in time with the beat.

Daughters remind fathers

to run around barefoot once in a while.

Fathers scoop up daughters

in their arms and say "I love you."

Fathers teach daughters

how to parallel park.

Daughters drive fathers

crazy sometimes.

Daughters show fathers

how to do a cartwheel.

Fathers teach daughters

to take care of their favorite toys.

Fathers encourage daughters

to express themselves.

Daughters teach fathers

proper tea party etiquette.

Daughters show fathers

their favorite places.

Fathers remind daughters

to take a moment and rest.

Fathers will recognize their daughters

no matter how much they change.

Daughters inspire fathers

to be imaginative.

Daughters hold on tightly

to fathers for reassurance.

Fathers encourage daughters

to appreciate nature's beauty.

Fathers introduce daughters

to the arts.

Daughters help fathers

be more patient.

Daughters believe

that their fathers
are Super Daddies.

Fathers show daughters

that Super Daddies are
experts at tying shoes.

Fathers teach daughters

to value friendships.

Daughters encourage fathers

to take the time to bond.

Daughters teach fathers

how to ask what's wrong.

Fathers give daughters

extra hugs when they're
having a tough day.

DANCING ON THE

A Story of an Atlantic Blue

by Kathleen M. Hollenbeck

SMITHSONIAN OCEAN

Fathers help daughters

with their homework.

Daughters remind fathers

how to do long division.

Fathers kiss daughters' boo-boos

to help them heal faster.

Daughters hug fathers

after a rough day at the office.

Fathers teach daughters
that there is always
time for dancing.
Daughters show fathers
new dance moves.

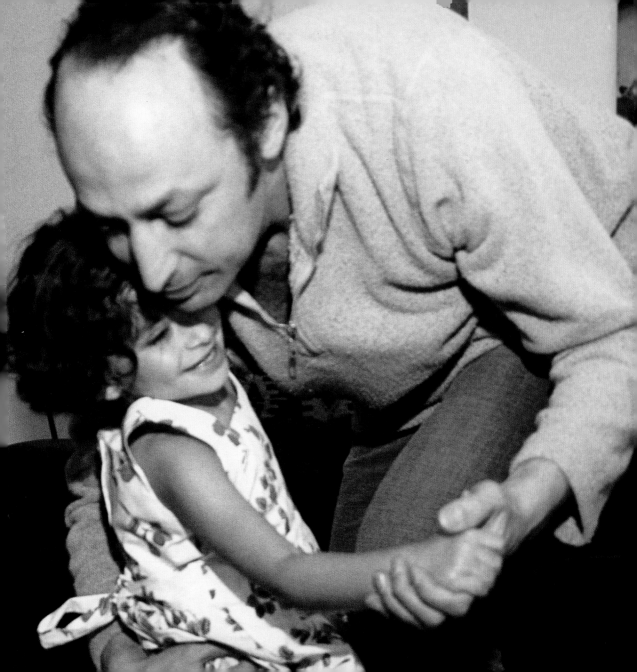

Daughters keep

their fathers company.

Fathers share

their favorite sport

with their daughters.

Fathers encourage daughters

to travel around the world.

Daughters know that fathers

will always be waiting

for them at home.

Daughters inspire fathers

to not be too serious.

Fathers tell daughters

"Beware of the Tickle Monster!"

Fathers teach daughters

that dads can play dress up, too.

Daughters show fathers

how to greet a princess.

Daughters love

working with fathers in the yard.

Fathers let daughters

decide which flowers go where.

Fathers teach daughters

how to wash the car.

Daughters help fathers

find all of the dirty spots.

Daughters remind fathers

to look for magic
in everyday moments.

Fathers teach daughters

to be confident heroines.

Fathers tell daughters

that they love them

even during disagreements.

Daughters know that fathers

want what is best for them.

Daughters teach fathers

how to celebrate birthdays in style.

Fathers show daughters

how to enjoy the spotlight.

Fathers give daughters

a special place in their hearts.

Daughters reassure fathers

that they will always be

"Daddy's little girl."

Daughters challenge fathers

to blinking contests.

Fathers try

to make daughters giggle.

Fathers encourage daughters

to take in their surroundings.

Daughters teach fathers

to enjoy the journey.

Photo Credits